A Mirror Image

by Z. J. Kentor

 HOUGHTON MIFFLIN   BOSTON

PHOTOGRAPHY CREDITS
Cover © Richard Walters/Visuals Unlimited; **1** © PhotoDisc; **3** © PhotoDisc; **5** © age fotostock/SuperStock; **6 Top Left** © istock photo; **6 Bottom left** © Corbis/Punch Stock; **6 Right** © Brand X Pictures/Punch Stock; **7** © Brand X Pictures/PunchStock; **9** © Richard Walters/Visuals Unlimited; **10–11** © Emely/zefa/Corbis; **11** © Digital Archive Japan/Punch Stock

Printed in China

ISBN 10: 0-618-89998-7
ISBN 13: 978-0-618-89998-2

11 12 13 14 15 0940 20 19 18 17 16 15

4500534964

Remember the first time you made a valentine for a classmate or someone in your family? First, you folded a sheet of red construction paper in half. Then you drew half a heart shape on it. Finally, you cut out the shape. When you unfolded the paper, you had a whole heart shape. The right and left sides looked exactly the same. That is because the shape you made had line symmetry.

If something is folded in half along a certain line, then it has line symmetry and the two sides match. This means that the two sides are congruent. The heart shape you made has one line of symmetry, or bilateral symmetry. You can only fold it one way (in half) for the sides to be congruent.

One of the best examples of bilateral symmetry can be found on a butterfly. Look closely at the wings of the butterfly in the picture on this page. The wing pattern on one side of the insect is the same as the wing pattern on the other side. This is bilateral symmetry. It is the mirror image of the other wing pattern. In other words, if you held a mirror along the body of the butterfly, you would see a reflection of one set of wings. This reflection would look exactly like the other set of wings.

Most insects have bilateral symmetry. Each side of an insect's body has one eye, three legs, and one antenna.

Read·Think·Write Look at the picture. In what ways are the butterfly's wings symmetrical?

After thinking about it, you have probably realized that most creatures in the animal kingdom have bilateral symmetry. Do you know why?

When both sides of an animal are equal, the animal can move more easily. How could a cheetah run fast if its left legs were shorter than its right legs? How could a monkey quickly swing through the trees if it had an arm on only one side?

What about people? People often say that a human's face is symmetrical. Is it really? The next time you are in front of a mirror, take a close look at your face. Is the left side identical to the right side? It probably is not. One side might have more freckles. Maybe you have a dimple on only one cheek. But it is so close to being identical that we often say the human face is symmetrical.

Read·Think·Write What can you find in this child's face that is not symmetrical?

When you look for it, you will find many other objects in nature that have bilateral symmetry. For example, pick up a tree leaf and fold it in half the long way. It may not be perfectly symmetrical, but like the human face, it is very close. What about sea shells? Have you ever seen a scallop shell at the beach? It is symmetrical. Crabs, lobsters, and many fish also have bilateral symmetry. If you could draw a straight line down their backs, you would find that each side mirrors the other. Much of what we find in nature has symmetry of one kind or another.

The Taj Mahal

Many objects that humans build also show symmetry. The Taj Mahal in India is a great example. Look at the picture of the Taj Mahal. If you ran a line down the middle of it, you would have bilateral symmetry.

Now look at the mirror image of the building in the water. Notice the line where the water begins to reflect the building. That is also a line of symmetry. This picture, then, has two lines of symmetry—one horizontal and one vertical.

Read·Think·Write What are the two lines of symmetry in the picture of the Taj Mahal?

Other objects or shapes may have two or more lines of symmetry. Look at the figures on this page. The red lines represent the lines of symmetry in each figure. If you fold any of the figures along one of the red lines, the two sides will match, or be congruent.

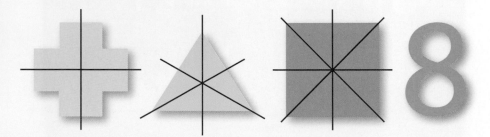

The first figure has two lines of symmetry. You can fold the figure two different ways and the opposite sides will match.

The second figure has three lines of symmetry. Each time you fold along one of the three fold lines, you get two matching sides.

The third figure has four lines of symmetry. You can fold the figure four different ways to get two matching sides.

Read·Think·Write How many lines of symmetry are in the number 8?

Now that we have looked at line symmetry, let's look at a second type of symmetry called rotational symmetry. When something has rotational symmetry, it can be rotated and still look the same. Snowflakes are a good example of rotational symmetry. Look at this snowflake. You can rotate it six different times and it looks the same each time.

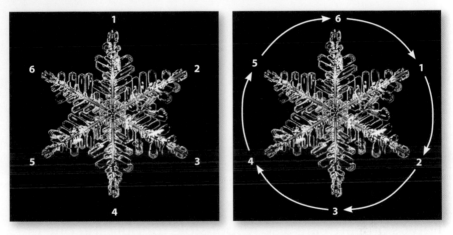

The number of times you can rotate an object and still have it look the same is called the order. A snowflake has an order of six.

Another example of rotational symmetry in nature is a starfish. How many times can you rotate a starfish and have it look the same? Five. So, a starfish has an order of five.

Read·Think·Write What are the two types of symmetry?

Do you like to eat honey? Honey comes from honeycombs. Bees make honeycombs. The same insects that turn nectar from flowers into one of the sweetest liquids on Earth are also responsible for building one of the most amazing structures ever. Look at this picture of a honeycomb. Can you see the symmetry?

Not only is each cell in a honeycomb symmetrical, but the ways the cells are connected are symmetrical as well. It is hard to believe that these little creatures can create something as complex as this.

Read·Think·Write How many lines of symmetry does each honeycomb cell have?

Did you know that symmetry can also affect how an insect behaves? For example, scientists have found that insects that get nectar from flowers seem to like flowers that are symmetrical more than ones that are not. This is probably because symmetrical flowers produce more pollen and nectar. These insects eat nectar to survive, and they spread pollen so plants can reproduce. It makes sense that they would be attracted to the flowers with the most to offer.

The next time you are outside, look for symmetry in the things around you. You may be amazed at what you find!

1. What type(s) of symmetry does this object have?

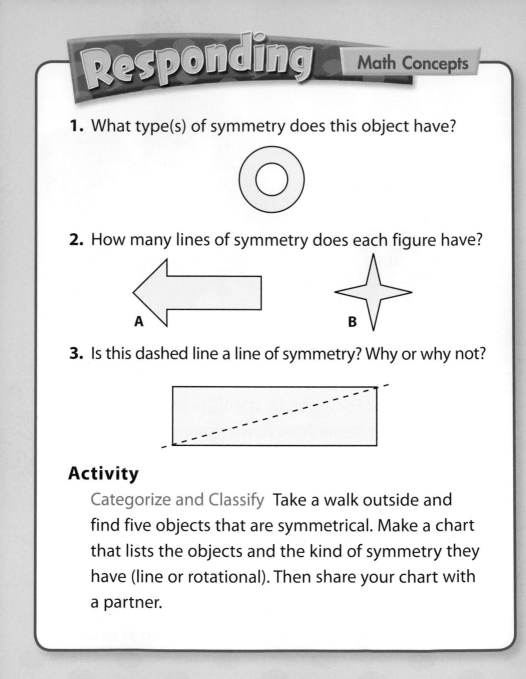

2. How many lines of symmetry does each figure have?

A

B

3. Is this dashed line a line of symmetry? Why or why not?

Activity

Categorize and Classify Take a walk outside and find five objects that are symmetrical. Make a chart that lists the objects and the kind of symmetry they have (line or rotational). Then share your chart with a partner.